00053539

306.08997
WEI

CANCELLED 2 1 MAR 2023

D0585377

AYLESBURY COLLEGE LEARNING CENTRE
OXFORD ROAD, AYLESBURY,
BUCKS. HP21 8PD
TEL: 01296 588588

Please return book on or before last date stamped below

GLOBAL CULTURES

American Indian Cultures

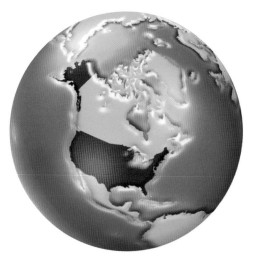

Ann Weil and Charlotte Guillain

www.raintreepublishers.co.uk
Visit our website to find out more information about Raintree books.

To order:
☎ Phone 0845 6044371
🖷 Fax +44 (0) 1865 312263
✉ Email myorders@raintreepublishers.co.uk

Customers from outside the UK please telephone +44 1865 312262

Raintree is an imprint of Capstone Global Library Limited, a company incorporated in England and Wales having its registered office at 7 Pilgrim Street, London, EC4V 6LB – Registered company number: 6695582

Text © Capstone Global Library Limited 2013
First published in hardback in 2013
The moral rights of the proprietor have been asserted.

All rights reserved. No part of this publication may be reproduced in any form or by any means (including photocopying or storing it in any medium by electronic means and whether or not transiently or incidentally to some other use of this publication) without the written permission of the copyright owner, except in accordance with the provisions of the Copyright, Designs, and Patents Act 1988 or under the terms of a licence issued by the Copyright Licensing Agency, Saffron House, 6–10 Kirby Street, London EC1N 8TS (www.cla.co.uk). Applications for the copyright owner's written permission should be addressed to the publisher.

Edited by Charlotte Guillain, Abby Colich, and Vaarunika Dharmapala
Designed by Steve Mead
Original illustrations © Capstone Global Library Ltd 2013
Illustrations by Oxford Designers & Illustrators
Picture research by Ruth Blair
Originated by Capstone Global Library Ltd
Printed and bound in China by Leo Paper Products Ltd

ISBN 978 1 406 24177 8 (hardback)
16 15 14 13 12
10 9 8 7 6 5 4 3 2 1

British Library Cataloguing in Publication Data
Weil, Ann.
American Indian cultures. --
306'.08997-dc23
A full catalogue record for
available from the British L

Acknowledgements
We would like to thank the following for permission to reproduce photographs: Alamy pp. 5 (© Chuck Place), 14 (© Nancy G. Western Photography, Nancy Greifenhagen), 19 (© Pat Canova), 22 (© Mike Dobel), 27 (© Anders Ryman), 31 (© Buddy Mays), 35 (© Ralph William), 37 (© Trinity Mirror/Mirrorpix), 41 (© David R. Frazier Photolibrary, Inc.); Corbis pp. 9 (© Peter Turnley), 11 (© Werner Forman), 12 (© Nathan Benn), 16 (© Maggie Steber/National Geographic Society), 18 (© Kerrick James), 20 (© Marilyn Angel Wynn/Nativestock Pictures), 23 (© Boomer Jerritt/All Canada Photos), 26 (© Bettmann), 30 (© Christopher Felver), 32 (© Marilyn Angel Wynn/Nativestock Pictures), 38 (© George H.H. Huey), 40 (© Danny Lehman); Dreamstime.com design features (© Aroas); Getty Images pp. 6 (Paul Chesley), 10 (National Geographic/Willard R. Culver); Photoshot pp. 7, 15, 17, 29 (© UPPA), 34 (© EPA), 36 (© WpN); Shutterstock pp. 8 (© Jim Feliciano), 13 (© Tomaz Kunst), 24 (© Dennis Donohue), 33 (© Alan C. Heison), 43 top left (© pr2is), 43 bottom left (© Doug James), 43 top right (© Steffen Foerster Photography), 43 bottom right (© J.L. Levy).

Cover photograph of a smiling American Indian boy reproduced with permission of Alamy (© John Cancalosi). Cover design feature of a colourful textile reproduced with permission of Dreamstime.com (© Aroas).

Every effort has been made to contact copyright holders of any material reproduced in this book. Any omissions will be rectified in subsequent printings if notice is given to the publisher.

Disclaimer
All the internet addresses (URLs) given in this book were valid at the time of going to press.

306.08997 WEI

AYLESBURY COLLEGE
LEARNING CENTRE

00053539

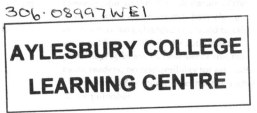

CONTENTS

Some words are shown in bold, **like this**. You can find out what they mean by looking in the glossary.

INTRODUCING AMERICAN INDIAN CULTURES

What do you know about American Indians? Perhaps you have seen a totem pole or a Navajo rug. Perhaps you have heard of certain tribes, such as the Cherokee, Sioux, and Apache.

American Indians are an important part of the history and **culture** of the United States. They lived there long before Europeans invaded and settled in the country, and developed their own flourishing societies. From the mid-1800s on, the US government forced many American Indians to live on **reservations**. Today, some choose to remain on reservations, while others live in towns and cities all over the country.

Did you know?

There are over 500 American Indian tribes in the United States, and American Indians make up 1.5 per cent of the population. The largest tribal groups include the Apache, Cherokee, Chippewa, Choctaw, Lumbee, Navajo, Pueblo, and Sioux.

What is culture?

Culture is the values, beliefs, and attitudes of a particular place and people. It is about how people live and worship, and about the music, art, and literature they produce. American Indians have never thought of themselves as one people with one culture. Each tribe developed their own beliefs, **customs**, languages, clothing, and homes over thousands of years.

This dancer from Tucson, Arizona is wearing his **traditional** clothes for a special celebration.

FAMILY AND SOCIETY

In different American Indian cultures, families and communities work and live together in different ways. For example, the Blackfeet in the northern Plains traditionally lived in a band made up of 80 to 240 people, living in 10 to 30 **lodges**. Each band had a leader who was chosen by the group.

In the south-eastern Cherokee culture, there are seven **clans**. Children become a member of their mother's clan. The Iroquois Confederacy is made up of six closely related tribes, with nine clans. Although modern life has affected the way many American Indians live, people still have a very strong connection to their tribe or nation.

These Blackfeet children live in Montana. The Blackfeet are well known to be brave warriors and excellent hunters.

Men's roles

Traditionally, American Indian men were warriors, **diplomats**, and hunters. Their main role was to protect, heal, and provide for their community. Men were also religious leaders. They led ceremonies to keep the people in harmony with natural and **spiritual** forces.

Plains Indians, such as the Cheyenne and Pawnee, depended on buffalo for food, clothes, and other necessities. Men tracked and killed the buffalo. Plains Indians also used horses, which had been introduced by the Spanish. Horses meant that people could travel over greater distances more easily.

This young Navajo is holding a coup stick made of cactus wood.

Men also rode into battle. A warrior's importance depended on his skill and bravery. The bravest among the warriors carried **coup** sticks. If they touched an enemy with the stick it was considered very brave. A notch was carved into the coup stick to record this bravery.

Women's roles

American Indian women have always gathered wild seeds, berries, and roots for food. They also look for herbs, used for healing. They know where to find these plants in the areas where they live.

In most cultures, women were traditionally in charge of the home, taking care of babies and young children. Blackfeet women not only looked after their homes but they built them, too. When their community, or band, moved to new land it was the women who carried the pieces of wood that made up their houses.

It is a woman's job to cut meat caught by the men into strips. Some is eaten fresh, but most is dried in the sun or cooked over a fire to make it last longer. Plains Indians, such as the Arapaho and Sioux, make pemmican by mixing pounded dried meat with fat and berries and then shaping it into cubes. In the past, pemmican was stored for use when **game** was scarce.

This is a *metate,* a stone instrument used by American Indian women for grinding corn or grain.

Women and leadership

Although American Indian leaders have traditionally been men, women have power, too. Among the Iroquois, women decide which men will be leaders. North-west coast women control how the tribe's money and land are used. In the Navajo culture, the women inherit their family's homes and rights to use land.

Wilma Pearl Mankiller (1945–2010)

Wilma Mankiller was the Cherokee Nation's first female Principal Chief. She held this office for 10 years, working hard to improve health and education for members of her tribe. She also built a strong relationship with the US government and was awarded the Presidential Medal of Freedom in 1998.

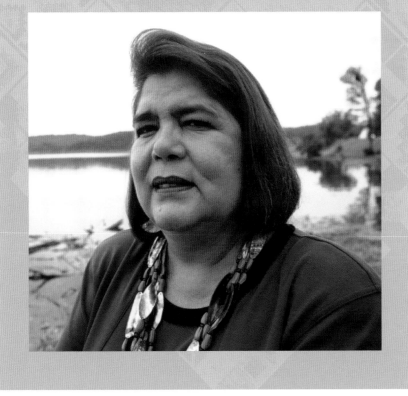

Transport

After the European invasion, many tribes were forced to leave their traditional homelands. Others were forced to accept small reservations instead of the large areas of land they once occupied. Before this, many tribes had moved within their lands, following the herds of animals they hunted and finding fresh grazing land.

This Seminole man is carving a canoe from cypress wood.

American Indians took all their belongings when they moved, including their homes. Algonquin people carried loads on toboggans. These long sledges were made of thin curved wood to move quickly over snow. The Iroquois made long canoes that could hold more than 15 people. The Lenape in Delaware used sledges and snowshoes in winter, canoes on water, and pack dogs over land.

Tools and weapons

Traditionally, American Indians made their tools from materials such as bone, stone, wood, and plants. When Europeans arrived in the 17th century, Indians traded for objects they could not make themselves.

One of the most prized trade goods was the gun.

American Indian tribes sometimes went to war. Weapons included bow and arrows and axe-like tomahawks. Lenape warriors used war clubs and carried shields made of hide and wood. Some Indians used shields to protect themselves. Shields were decorated to make them powerful.

Did you know?

Choctaw people in Oklahoma hunt wild game today, usually using guns. In the past, Choctaw hunters used specially designed hunting tools. They used hollowed-out canes as blow guns to kill birds and small animals. Rabbit sticks were carved wooden clubs that were thrown hard at small game.

Warriors believed a shield's power helped protect them in battle.

Homes

Most American Indians live in modern houses today, but many keep traditional homes like their **ancestors** had. The Plains Indians, such as the Blackfeet, Comanche, and Cheyenne, traditionally lived in tent-like **tipis** covered in buffalo skins. The women took down and rebuilt the tipis when the group moved. Families today may take a tipi to festivals and gatherings.

Did you know?

Many people believe that all American Indians were **nomads** who lived in tipis. This image has been created by films, television, and books. In fact, American Indians have many different traditional homes. All groups had their own settlements and moved to and from these throughout the year.

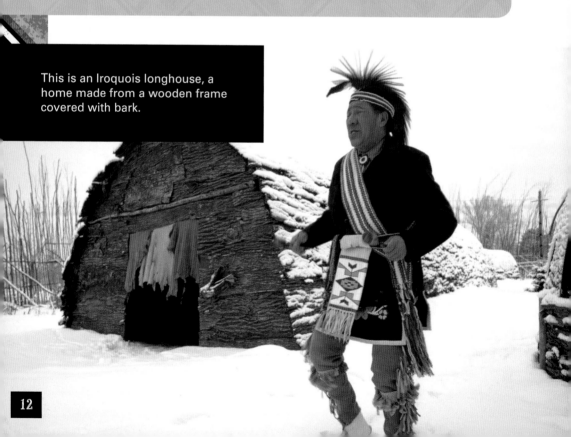

This is an Iroquois longhouse, a home made from a wooden frame covered with bark.

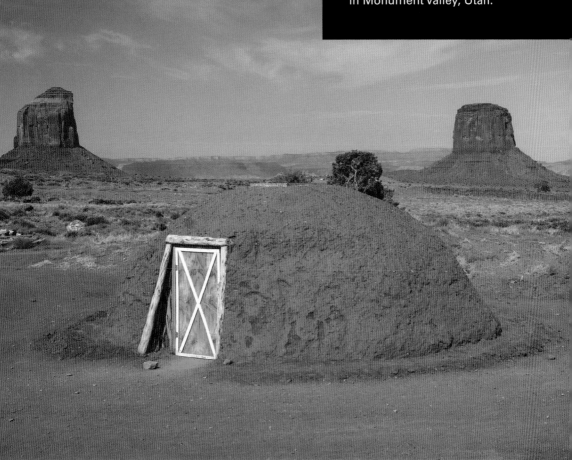

These Navajo *hogans* are in Monument Valley, Utah.

In other cultures, different types of home depended on the environment and local materials. The traditional Navajo dwelling in the south-west was an eight-sided *hogan*. It was made from logs and mud with an earth roof. The Penobscot in the north-east lived in small birchbark houses called wigwams.

Apaches lived in huts called *wickiups* made from arched poles covered with bark, grass, or branches. These structures were easy to take apart and carry from place to place. North-west coast Indians lived in sturdy plank houses while the Seminoles in Florida lived in log cabins. After moving to swampy areas, they lived in structures called *chickees* with floors raised up above the water.

ORNAMENT

Beauty is part of everything in American Indian life. Everyone creates beautiful objects, making items that people in a **Western** culture would call art.

Clothing

Today, most people, including American Indians, buy their clothes in shops. In the past, American Indians made everything they wore from materials they could find nearby or obtain through trade. Some American Indians were hunters who made clothes from animal skins. The Iroquois tribes hunted deer, so they made clothes from **tanned** buckskin. The Plains Indians, such as the Sioux and Blackfeet tribes, hunted buffalo and made warm robes from buffalo skins.

Some American Indians made clothes from plants woven together to make cloth. The Pueblo Indian tribes in the south-west were farmers who made clothes from cotton.

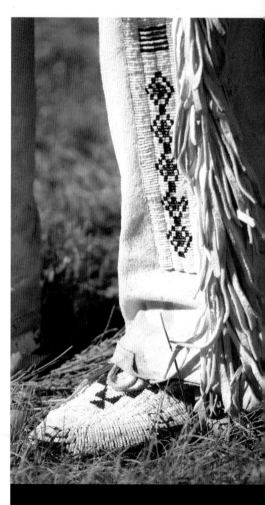

Traditionally, many American Indian men wore a **breech cloth** and decorated leggings, such as these worn by a Sioux man.

Most American Indians today wear the same kinds of clothes as other Americans or Europeans. Like most other cultures, many American Indians wear traditional styles of clothing for festivals, ceremonies, and other special occasions that celebrate their **heritage**.

Did you know?

Moccasins are soft leather shoes worn by many American Indian groups. Different tribes cut the leather and decorate their moccasins in different ways. The Ojibwe moccasins below are made from moosehide and decorated with beads.

The name Blackfeet is a translation of the word *siksika*. This described the dark moccasins the Blackfeet Indians wore.

Body paint

Many American Indian warriors painted their faces, bodies, and horses before going into battle. They believed this gave them protection. Others wore body paint for **rituals**. Each paint colour had its own special meaning. Seminoles, for example, wore red paint during wartime and white paint during peace time. When several tribes got together, each group could be identified by its body paint and clothing.

Today, American Indians, such as this Cherokee man, may wear face and body paint just as their ancestors did at celebrations and festivals.

Beadwork

American Indians use small shells, feathers, and porcupine quills to decorate clothes, moccasins, and other items. Some also make beads from materials such as precious stones, found where they live. For example, tribes in the south-west, such as the Navajo and Apache, use turquoise beads in their jewellery and decoration. Today, small glass beads are commonly used for decoration. These were introduced by Europeans around 500 years ago.

Each American Indian culture develops new patterns. Kiowa women owned the designs they created. This meant no one else could copy it without the owner's permission.

This Ojibwe bag is decorated with geometric patterns.

YOUNG PEOPLE

Some groups of American Indians, such as the Cheyenne, make beaded pouches, often in the shape of animals such as turtles. These are used to contain a piece of a baby's **umbilical cord** after he or she is born. The child can then keep the pouch for good luck.

Weaving

Members of the Coast Salish tribes on the north-west coast still wear blanket robes as their ancestors did in the past. Traditionally, these blankets were woven from the hair of mountain goats.

Sheep were introduced to the south-west by the Spanish about 400 years ago. The Navajo people began raising sheep for wool, which they used to weave blankets. These blankets have become famous for their beauty. The patterns often include brightly coloured geometric shapes and zig-zags. Weavers used light tools, and often wove outside where there was plenty of light and space to work.

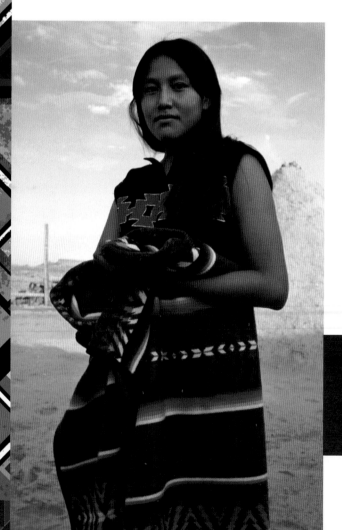

Baskets were another woven household item. Many cultures, including the Pomos, Apaches, and Algonquins, used grasses and strips of tree bark to make baskets.

Today, most Navajo women learn how to weave.

Pottery

Many cultures use clay to make containers to hold food, water, and objects. American Indians in different regions used their local clay to make pottery. Groups in the Mississippi valley made pots shaped like people. Other groups made coil pots, using long tubes of clay coiled into the shape of a container. Different cultures decorated pottery in various ways. For example, in the south-west, the Mimbres people painted their pottery with animal designs, while the Mogollon culture used spiral patterns.

American Indians still make pots today but now they are mostly sold to tourists and collectors, or used on special occasions.

Maria Montoya Martinez (1887–1980)

The Pueblo Indian Maria Montoya Martinez was an artist and potter who lived in New Mexico. She learned a traditional method of making coil pots and used ancient techniques to fire (bake) and glaze (cover in a shiny coating) her work. Her deep black pottery made her famous around the world.

This bowl was made by the Hopi people of Arizona.

BELIEFS AND CEREMONY

American Indian cultures do not separate religion from everyday life the way people of other cultures do. Instead, they express their religion in almost everything they do. Traditionally, hunting was sacred, or holy. American Indians believed the animal **sacrificed** its body so the people could eat. They believe the land is sacred. Some Indian **creation stories** describe particular places. These stories tell how each group of people came to be on their land, along with the animals and plants that also live there.

Medicine wheels represent harmony, and are used for rituals, healing, and teaching. They are always made up of white, yellow, red, and black stones.

For many American Indians, there are three stages in a person's life that have a strong spiritual significance: birth, becoming an adult, and death. Some tribes perform special rituals at the place where a baby is born. That place is then sacred to the person, and remains important throughout his or her life. This spiritual connection to the land was one reason American Indians suffered so much when they were forced to live on reservations, sometimes away from their homeland.

Even war was sacred. When they went to war, warriors used special sacred words instead of speaking the way they would at home. Many believed their ancestors' spirits continued to live after their bodies had died.

Medicine bundles are an important part of Blackfeet Indians' spiritual life. These are bundles of items needed for a special ritual or ceremony, wrapped in cloth or hide. They could contain anything from herbs, paint, clothing, or tools. The Blackfeet believe these bundles have power when used in particular rituals and special ceremonies are held to pass them on to someone new.

Did you know?

The spirit world is an important part of American Indian life. American Indians believe that all things, including animals, humans, and plants, have a spirit. People pray and carry out special rituals to connect with these spirits and try to achieve balance in their life. Some rituals involve telling creation stories. It is considered important to show great respect for the natural world.

Totem poles

North-west coast peoples make totem poles. Totem poles are tall structures carved out of cedar wood. Many have images of animals, such as bears and birds, carved into the wood. The images often tell creation stories, or describe the history of a powerful family. The poles were put in front of people's lodges and were often brightly painted. Today, skilled American Indian artists carve new poles for museums and collectors and teach the art to new generations.

Masks

In many American Indian cultures, masks are an important part of rituals and ceremonies. North-west coast Indians carve masks out of wood. The masks can show spirits, famous ancestors, or animals. People believe the tree sacrificed part of itself so the people could have the mask. They believe that just as a tree was alive, so is the mask. The masks are still worn when stories are told and some have moveable pieces to change the wearer's voice or expression.

The tallest totem poles can be over 15 metres (49 feet) high.

The Navajo and Apache peoples in the South-West made masks from leather, while the Cherokee used decorated **gourds**. These masks are used during storytelling.

Masks were treated as living things by the people who made them.

Did you know?

The Iroquois of the north-east have a ceremony where an ancient story is told. Members of the "False Face Society" put on masks and look for sick members of their community to heal. These painted wooden masks are considered to be sacred and living representations of spirits.

Ceremonies and rituals

All American Indian cultures have special ceremonies and rituals. These might involve dances, gatherings, and storytelling. Different groups show respect for different spirits or animals. For example, the owl and cougar are special to Cherokees in the south-east because they are in their creation story. Many groups hold ceremonies to give thanks for the natural world around them.

Great New Moon Ceremony

In the Cherokee culture, the Great New Moon Ceremony was celebrated in autumn. The Cherokees believe the world was created at this time of year. People gathered to share food and dance. The celebration was a way to give thanks to their Creator. Some Cherokees still observe this festival today.

Sun Dance

The Sun Dance is a Sioux religious ceremony. During this ritual, men shed their blood to show thanks. They use sharp bones and sticks to pierce their upper body. Sun Dancers enter a **trance** and they may have **visions**. This provides guidance for their tribe.

In 1883, the US government outlawed Sun Dances, as well as a number of other American Indian religious practices. This decision was reversed in 1934. Today, Sun Dances are held on some Sioux reservations during the summer.

YOUNG PEOPLE

In the Blackfeet culture, young people use a vision quest to connect with the spirit world. They go to an isolated place, such as a mountain, and **fast**. This makes them weaker and they may have a vision.

A vision quest helps young people discover their own personal animal spirit guide, which could be a bear, buffalo, coyote, wolf, or any other creature. Blackfeet believe this animal spirit helps the person throughout his or her life.

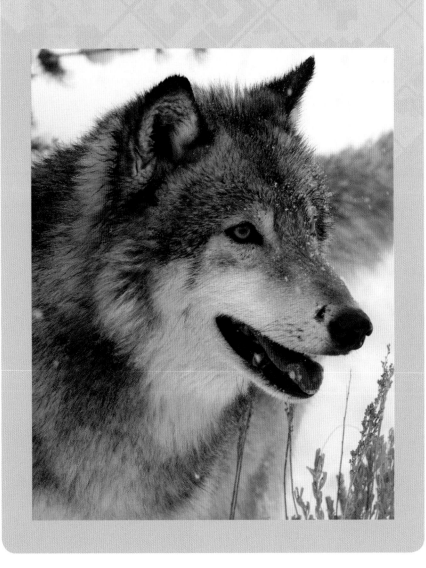

Rites of passage

A rite of passage is a sacred act performed to celebrate when a person moves from one life stage to another. Birth, becoming an adult, marriage, and death are all rites of passage. American Indians had rituals for many life changes, such as when a person became a leader. Some of these rituals are still continued today.

Names

Northern Plains Indian men used to get new names with each new life stage to reflect their activities or personality. It is thought that the famous Lakota chief known as Sitting Bull was called Jumping Badger when he was born. After his first success in battle, his father gave him the name Sitting Bull. This had been the father's warrior name.

Sitting Bull helped his people gain victory against the US Army at the Battle of the Little Bighorn in 1876.

Sunrise Dance

Western Apache girls mark the beginning of their womanhood with a Sunrise Dance. The girl's godmother dresses her for the ceremony. The community sings songs about Changing Woman from the Apache creation story. The girl dances to the songs, stepping gently from one foot to the other. This ritual gives her the physical and spiritual strength of Changing Woman. She also practises skills she will need as an adult.

This Apache girl is taking part in the Sunrise Dance. She is painted in sacred clay and corn meal.

YOUNG PEOPLE

In American Indian hunter and warrior societies, manhood traditionally came after boys took part in a successful hunt or had their first experience in battle. Today, many young American Indian men do **military service** to prove their manhood.

DAILY LIFE AND CUSTOMS

American Indians traditionally ate local plants and meat from animals they hunted. Acorn mush was a popular dish among American Indians in California. It took hours of work to grind the acorns and get rid of their bitter taste by soaking them in hot water.

Many American Indians described months and seasons according to what could be eaten at that time. They held festivals to celebrate important foods.

Green Corn Festival

The Green Corn Festival is a Pueblo tradition that continues today. "Green corn" is ripe and ready to eat. People celebrate a good harvest with dancing and feasting, and give thanks to their creator. Green corn is delicious but they leave most cobs on the stalk so it dries. They harvest the dried corn later and use it to make corn meal, which they can eat all winter.

Did you know?

Eastern and Woodland Indians grew corn, squash, and beans. These three food crops were a very important part of their diet. They were called the "Three Sisters" by tribes such as the Iroquois and Wampanoag because they grew well together and were often eaten together in a dish called succotash.

These Navajo girls are demonstrating how corn is traditionally ground. They are using special stones called a *mano* and a *metate*.

Potlatch

North-west coast Indians have a giveaway ceremony called a potlatch. *Potlatch* comes from a word that means "to give". American Indian leaders need to show generosity to increase their status.

In a potlatch, the host serves more food than guests can finish. Salmon is the traditional food, along with berries, seaweed, and meat. After the feast, guests take leftovers and gifts home with them. The host might also give away blankets and other goods as gifts.

Storytelling

In the past, American Indians did not have books. They told stories instead. This was how history and culture were passed on from one generation to the next. All American Indian cultures have creation stories. These stories tell how Earth was formed and how the people came to live where they were. There are also stories that tell how animals came to be the way they are. In some, animals talk and act like people. Some of these tales have a message at the end, and help teach children how to behave properly.

Joseph Bruchac (born 1942)

Joseph Bruchac is a storyteller and author. Some of his ancestors were Abenaki Indians in the north-east and much of his work reflects his American Indian roots. He has written books for both children and adults. He is also a professional storyteller, retelling the traditional stories of the north-eastern Woodlands peoples.

Some stories were told only at certain times of the year. Storytellers had to learn their craft carefully, because stories had to be told the same way each time.

Cochiti storyteller dolls

The Cochiti are Pueblo Indians who live in New Mexico. Helen Cordero (1915–1994) was a Cochiti Indian who wanted to preserve her tribe's storytelling traditions and remember her storytelling grandfather. She began sculpting clay figures of storytellers sharing traditional tales with children in 1964.

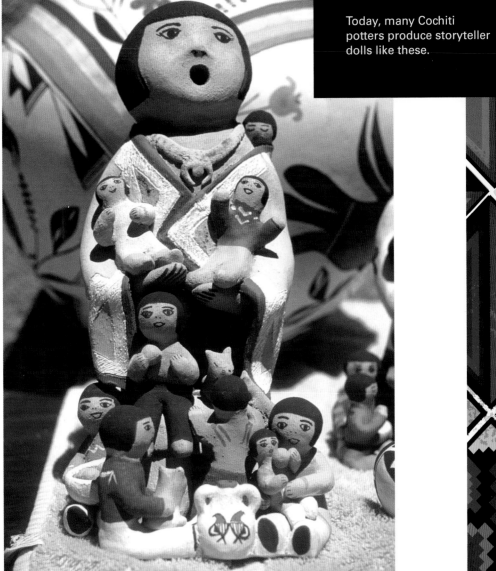

Today, many Cochiti potters produce storyteller dolls like these.

Toys

Many traditional American Indian toys and games helped children understand their own world and the sacred world. Some tribes played a ring and pin game, where a ring or bundle of twigs is attached to a cord. This is thrown in the air and then caught on the pin. On the south-west coast, tribes such as the Zuni batted a shuttlecock made of corn and feathers with their hands. Many toys had religious importance.

Dolls

Many American Indian dolls help children learn about and respect their way of life. Some dolls are very simple. For example, Iroquois cornhusk dolls have no faces. This was to discourage vanity. The Iroquois believed that the corn spirit in the doll would choose which face to show the child.

These faceless cornhusk dolls are dressed in buckskin clothes.

The Havasupai in Arizona have made dolls from split twigs for thousands of years. The Hopi of New Mexico make *kachina* dolls. *Kachinas* stand for the life spirit of all things. They are used to teach children complicated stories about the spirit world and important Hopi traditions.

The Iroquois invented the game lacrosse, and today there is an Iroquois National team in the United States. The game is also played at some schools and colleges in the United States.

YOUNG PEOPLE

Long ago, Apache villages were often attacked by other tribes. Children played games to help them learn how to hide from these enemies. Apache boys played a kind of dodge ball. Instead of a ball, they dodged rocks and untipped arrows. They needed to learn how to dodge weapons to become skilled warriors.

PERFORMANCE

Music and dance are important for many American Indian peoples. Like other cultures around the world, groups get together to dance socially. Other dances have religious importance or are performed at traditional festivals.

Powwows

Powwows are a tradition that has grown during the last 100 years. A powwow is a big, multi-tribal gathering and celebration. It is a chance for both Indians and non-Indians to experience various cultures first-hand. American Indian foods and treats, such as fry bread (dough fried in oil), are offered for sale. Artists bring traditional and modern crafts for show and sale. Some "contest powwows" offer participants a chance to win big cash prizes.

These Sioux dancers are taking part in a powwow.

The world's largest gathering of American Indians is a powwow that takes place every year in Albuquerque, New Mexico. In April 2011, more than 3,000 American Indian singers and dancers performed over three days to huge crowds.

YOUNG PEOPLE

Powwows are an opportunity for young people to explore and express their traditions and cultural heritage. Young singers and dancers perform and compete at powwows wearing the **regalia** of their individual tribes. Some regalia combine symbols in new ways. Children getting involved in this way shows how American Indian cultures change with the times.

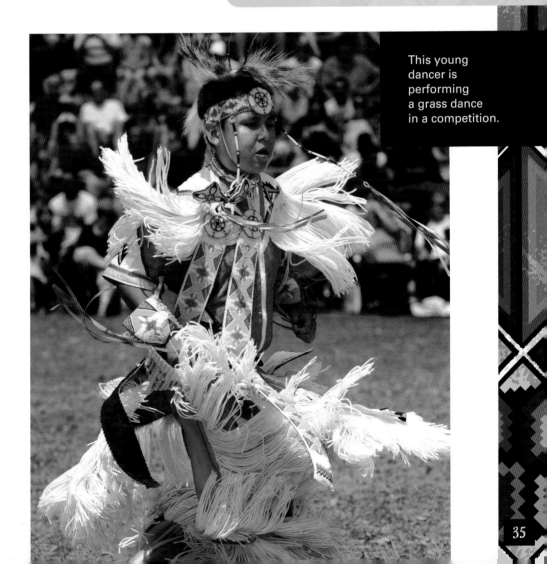

This young dancer is performing a grass dance in a competition.

Dance

American Indians dance to honour their cultures and ancestors and each other. It is another way they express their identity as native peoples. Like storytelling, dancing is a way to pass traditions down from one generation to the next.

Young Hopi people take part in a Butterfly dance in late summer. They dance in pairs and are accompanied by singers. The girls wear colourful headdresses called *kopatsoki*, which are made by their partners. The dance is performed to ask for rain and a happy, healthy life.

The Tohono O'odham people in the south-east dance to fiddle music. Their dances include a circle dance called a *kwariya*, which is performed by couples linked in a chain.

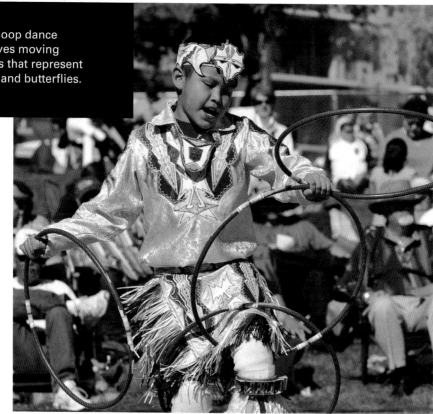

The hoop dance involves moving hoops that represent birds and butterflies.

Maria Tallchief (born 1925)

Maria Tallchief was born into a wealthy Osage family in 1925. She began studying ballet at the age of four. Her family moved from their reservation to Beverly Hills, California, so she could study with the best teachers. Maria performed her first solo dance at 15 and soon became a professional ballerina. Maria Tallchief was the first American Indian prima ballerina, starring in ballets in the United States and Europe.

Animal dances

Many American Indian dances reflect the importance and movement of animals. The Ho-Chunk people of the Great Lakes have dances that show the flight of geese and swans. The Iroquois are famous for their buffalo and bear dances, while several Pueblo tribes in the south-east perform deer dances.

Musical instruments

Rattles, flutes, and drums are the most important American Indian instruments. Instruments are made from wood, gourds, turtle shells, deer hooves, and other natural materials.

The Yaqui people of the south-west perform deer songs. A deer dancer wears rattles on his legs and ankles and may also carry hand rattles made from gourds.

Drums

North-west coastal peoples make beautifully painted drums that are hit with a beater. The paintings on the drums often show scenes from creation stories or important animals.

This is a ceremonial Navajo drum.

The Cochiti people of the south-west make drums from sections of hollow tree trunks. Leather is laced around the two ends to produce a distinctive sound when struck.

The Iroquois people play water drums. Water is placed inside the wooden drum and the drumskin is soaked to make it tighter. The water changes the sound that the drum makes.

Did you know?

Some tribes, such as the Kaw people of the Southern Plains and the Chippewa in the north, have special drumkeepers. The keepers are responsible for the care of the drums. To them, drums are not just objects, but are spiritual beings. To many American Indians, drumming represents the heartbeat of Mother Earth.

Singing

Like storytelling, singing is another way American Indians pass down their history. Singing is regarded as a form of prayer. For many American Indians it is one of the most sacred forms of expression.

Stories are put into songs so that new generations can remember them correctly. Some songs, such as lullabies, are enjoyed as part of everyday life, while other songs are more religious. American Indians communicate with the spirit world and the Creator through singing.

Some songs are so sacred that they can only be sung by certain people at certain times. In other American Indian cultures, people have the right to sing certain songs, and they are also allowed to sell them to other singers.

AMERICAN INDIAN CULTURES IN THE 21ST CENTURY

There is no single American Indian culture. During the 1800s, the US government tried to force American Indians to mix with the rest of the population. Many American Indians were forced to live on reservations, some of which were far from their traditional homeland. Many homelands contained precious resources that the government wanted. They outlawed some of the Indians' religious practices and it became difficult to follow traditional ways of life. American Indians were forced to adapt. Their various cultures today, like other modern cultures, are a mixture of past and present, growing and changing as they move into the future.

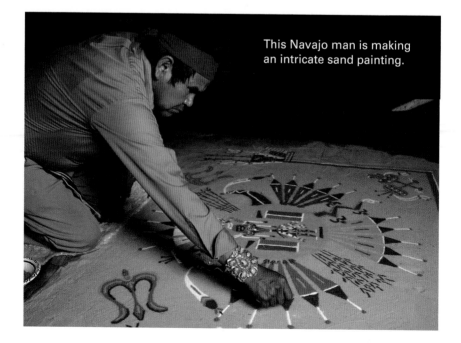

This Navajo man is making an intricate sand painting.

This museum display includes a large birchbark canoe.

Museums

Millions of objects from American Indians' past are preserved in museum collections. This gives people a chance to see everyday items such as moccasins and clothes, tools and weapons, jewellery, and other beautiful creations. Unfortunately, some of these objects were stolen from their rightful owners and many American Indians were upset that their belongings were in museums. Today, some museums are changing the way they handle and display American Indians' cultural heritage. They invite American Indians to share their knowledge so that the public can get a better understanding of traditional American Indian art and culture.

Through dance, art, storytelling, food, and pride in their heritage, American Indians of all cultures continue to express themselves, their people, and their place in the world today.

TIMELINE

BCE

18,000–15,000   Scientists believe the first American Indians arrive in North America from Siberia

CE

1492   Christopher Columbus lands in the West Indies

1565   Spanish colonists set up the first European settlement in present-day Florida

1620   English colonists settle in Massachusetts and receive help from local tribes

1838   Most south-eastern tribes are forced to move to reservations. This is known as "the Trail of Tears". Some Seminoles hide in swamplands to avoid being moved.

1870s–1880s   Plains Indians are forced to move to reservations

1887   The Dawes Act divides up American Indian land in an attempt to make the tribes adapt to white society

1887   Pueblo potter Maria Montoya Martinez is born

1925   Dancer Maria Tallchief is born

1942   Writer and storyteller Joseph Bruchac is born

1960s   American Indian communities start to protest past wrongs and celebrate their cultures

1964   Helen Cordero starts to make Cochiti dolls

1985   Wilma Mankiller becomes the Cherokee Nation's first female Principal Chief

2004   The National Museum of the American Indian opens in Washington DC

CULTURAL MAP

Totem pole

Mask

0   800 kilometres

0   500 miles

0   400   800 kilometres

0   250   500 miles

N

Powwow

Ojibwe wigwam

GLOSSARY

ancestor family relation from a very long time ago, such as a great-great-grandparent

breech cloth strip of material worn between the legs and held up with a belt

clan group of families or villages that share a common culture

coup blow or strike. Some tribes counted coup, or the number of times a warrior touched an enemy during battle.

creation story story that explains how an American Indian culture began

culture customs, social organisation, and achievements of a particular nation, people, or group

custom way things have been done for a long time

diplomat person skilled in keeping good relations between various individuals and groups

fast to go without food or drink for a certain length of time

game wild animals that are hunted for food

gourd large fleshy fruit with a hard skin

heritage anything from the past handed down by tradition

lodge type of American Indian home, lived in by extended families

military service time spent working in the armed forces

nomad person who has no fixed home, who moves from one place to another for much of the year

regalia traditional clothing worn during ceremonies

reservation piece of land set aside by the US government for American Indians, sometimes far away from the tribes' original homes

ritual formal actions in a ceremony

sacrifice when something, often a slaughtered animal, is offered to God

spiritual to do with religion and holy things

tan make animal skin into leather, usually by soaking in a special substance such as a solution of oak bark

tipi cone-shaped tent made of animal hides or bark

tradition customs that are passed on from one generation to the next

trance partially conscious state, when a person does not respond to anyone or anything

umbilical cord cord that connects a baby to its mother before birth

vision kind of dream that holds meaning

Western countries and societies that are economically developed

FIND OUT MORE

Books

California Indians, Liz Sonneborn (Heinemann, 2012)

Great Basin Indians, Melissa McDaniel (Heinemann, 2012)

North American Indian, David Hamilton Murdoch
  (Dorling Kindersley, 2005)

Northwest Coast Indians, Liz Sonneborn (Heinemann, 2012)

Plains Indians, Andrew Santella (Heinemann, 2012)

Plateau Indians, Christin Ditchfield (Heinemann, 2012)

Southeast Indians, Andrew Santella (Heinemann, 2012)

Southwest Indians, Melissa McDaniel (Heinemann, 2012)

The Girl Who Helped Thunder and Other Native American Folktales,
  James and Joseph Bruchac (Sterling Juvenile, 2009)

The United States of America (Countries Around the World),
  Michael Hurley (Raintree, 2012)

Websites

www.josephbruchac.com
Visit this website to find out more about Joseph Bruchac's
writing and storytelling.

Visit the following websites to find out more about some
of the tribes mentioned in this book:
www.blackfeetnation.com
www.cherokee.org
www.kawnation.com
www.lumbeetribe.com
www.navajo-nsn.gov
www.sioux.org

Places to visit

The British Museum, London

www.britishmuseum.org

Visit the North American gallery at the British Museum to see objects from a variety of American Indian cultures.

Horniman Museum, London

www.horniman.ac.uk

The Horniman Museum contains many American Indian objects.

The Pitt Rivers Museum, Oxford

www.prm.ox.ac.uk

See American Indian masks, clothes, canoes, and totem poles among other artefacts here.

If you ever get the chance to go to the United States, this is a place you could visit:

The National Museum of the American Indian

www.nmai.si.edu

Visit this museum to find out about the many and diverse American Indian cultures.

More topics to research

What topic did you like reading about most in this book? Did you find out anything that you thought was particularly interesting? Choose a topic that you liked, such as food, art, or religion, and try to find out more about it. You could visit one of the places mentioned above, have a look at one of the websites, or visit your local library to do some research. Topics to think about include Sitting Bull and the Battle of the Little Big Horn (1876), the Dawes Act (1887), and how to make a wigwam!

INDEX